Consciousness Detoured

Written by: Miladine Etienne

A Molding Messengers Publication

Consciousness Detoured
Copyright © 2020 by Miladine Etienne

All rights reserved. Printed in the United States of America. No part of this book may be used or reproduced in any manner whatsoever without written permission except in the case of brief quotations embodied in critical articles or reviews.
This book is a work of fiction. Names, characters, businesses, organizations, places, events and incidents either are the product of the author's imagination or are used fictitiously. Any resemblance to actual persons, living or dead, events, or locales is entirely coincidental.

For information about permission to reproduce selections from this book, Write to Molding Messengers, LLC 1728 NE Miami Gardens Dr, Suite #111, North Miami Beach, FL, 33179 or email Info.Staff@MoldingMessengers.com

Library of Congress Control Number: 2019915480
Print ISBN: 978-0-578-63536-1
Ebook ISBN: 978-0-578-63537-8

A Molding Messengers Publication

Consciousness Detoured

Written by: Miladine Etienne

A Molding Messengers Publication

Table of Contents

TEACHERS .... Page 1

NEW JEWS .... Page 3

BROKEN .... Page 5

DESTINATION .... Page 9

RIP .... Page 17

GOD .... Page 18

DETOUR .... Page 20

HUSBAND .... Page 22

NIGHTMARE .... Page 24

LIFETIME .... Page 25

FAMILY .... Page 27

RECIPROCITY .... Page 28

HAITIAN .... Page 29

CONTRARY .... Page 30

LIFE .... Page 32

BIRTHDAY .... Page 34

TED TALK .... Page 37

SAY .... Page 42

IF .... Page 44

MR. TIN-MAN .... Page 47

ME TOO .... Page 49

ANOTHER TRUTH .... Page 51

AGAIN .... Page 52

BOTH .... Page 53

FLESH .... Page 55

ME .... Page 56

WELL DONE .... Page 59

BROTHER .... Page 62

Preface

This body of work that I have had the opportunity to create is a tumultuous force. The timing that went into it (over ten years), the lives lost and gained, the failures, the triumphs and duplicating as much good as possible. I invite you to a new beginning and pray that you will not only read my words but live them independently allowing the words to live on infinitely.

TEACHERS

We're a peculiar crew...
We've been branded through
scars but they love us.
C'mon, come and tell us how to
love our jobs—love our students
and love the care we give.
We already know we're different.
We are a carry-it-all crew.
We've danced around our smiles.
Shot daggers through metal-filed
teeth but we love them...our
children, our patients.
We're the no-amount-of-money-
would-ever-be-enough-crew.

We do it because we love them and we see kings and queens in them even though they're humongous kids.
We're a peculiar crew, we carry them with us, they force us to be better, to live with care…
We are the mothers, family, friends, caregivers and educators.
We see them and love them.
We're the peculiar crew.

- M.E

NEW JEWS

We're like the people lost in
Egypt.
We ask for more not knowing
what it entails.
We wander to our own musings
and we curse ourselves without
truly knowing that time is a
Limited reversal of fluidity not
ease.
It moves like the ripples in water
caused by a pebble.
Kicked by a passerby on a gravel
road.

We're fickle people.
We complain and we are undone:
imperfect.

- M.E

BROKEN

Hello, I'm broken...
Wait before you begin to refute
me and hurl unwanted words of
wisdom in my direction.
Let me be that way for a while.
If not, I won't know how true
healing begins.
Haven't you ever felt cast aside,
unworthy, unseen?
Hello, I'm broken. Hello to you,
hello to me.
Hello, I'm broken.
Wait before you begin to deny

my present truth with your advice
to "look on the bright side..."
Let me be.
Haven't you ever felt so lost? So
much so that only the way, the
truth, and the light could bring
you back?
I'm broken.
It's a detour, not a destination.
Broken: it's a present, not a future
and far from past.
I'm broken and I KNOW only my
maker, the potter, can fix that.

- M.E

Shout Out to the Women of A Certain Age podcast! I know these beautiful, caring, God fearing women! These women are God loving, Holy Spirit filled and life goals oriented. They are really mentors unraveling life like a lot of us. Something I learned on one of their podcast episodes, helped me title this book. I've learned through listening to their show, that destinations aren't the main act, sometimes detours are abundantly necessary. Thank you W.O. C. A!

DESTINATION

I went into the first day of work scared shitless. But I needed a job, I needed money so I thought I'd stay as long as it took to build an honest savings account, make a dent in Sallie Mae's loan repayment program, and be an adult.

I did everything that I was supposed to and I interacted with the children. They were hard to ignore.

All bright faced and curious as to my role in their
lives; my role period.
So, I stayed.
The next couple of weeks were just me immersing myself in their world. Becoming a non-threatening fixture first, light interaction second, then full-on teacher third. Could they learn? Was it any use to them if they did? Am I going to get more MS exacerbations? I had no answers but I was determined not to be incapable or desolate. I was determined to work.

There came a time in my training where I had to work with the "gifted" students. Students whose "gifts" were elopement, pushing through doors with fire alarms, gutter-mouth-baiting, and a myriad of sanitary issues. Oh, those sanitary issues become an issue you pray for after six months of working with the children and being qualified to move onto "the best gifted child" or "gifted class."

I honestly didn't want a "thank you."

Those words were just words to me after I sprinted across the neighboring homes in a very well-kept neighborhood . They were just a mumble when I held onto a child as they were falling apart at the seams of their reality. But I could've used a higher pay. Not exorbitant but a decent wage. It would've been amazing to hear "...we're fighting with the company to get you all more money..." rather than "just get another part time job."

By then a "thank you" would've been a slap to the face but my coworkers still wanted it.
 I didn't blame them but I could not care less.
Meanwhile, I fell in love with the kids. That wasn't supposed to happen. I was there to work and get a paycheck. They weren't supposed to inadvertently teach me. My co-workers weren't supposed to be family. Those children taught me more about life and joy than any position I've held. I learned that

communication is a tremendous resource taken for granted. I learned forgiveness (because "K" doesn't care when or where he wants to push the alarmed door, he just does), I learned how important it is to be seen as a friend through "Y's" eyes than a disciplinarian. I learned more patience with myself than I ever did. I loved them and I loved myself so much so that I left the dismal paying position and sought out looking for a better one.

Taking all I learned from the children and peculiar people to a better valued position. No amount of money can give genuine care. That sincerity and love comes when the caregiver sees themselves in the person they're providing care for. Maybe that's what made me hold on to the job as long as I did. Children with disabilities hold mirrors in their eyes and beg you to love.

- M.E

RIP

Let me fall apart

Decimate into the finest powder

Crumble even and roll into my

Father's hands

Because only He can put me back

together again

Let me...let me topple over

Lose my footing

Let me grieve...yes for now...

Let me be.

- M.E

GOD

You were present in the children's
giggles, they're clumsy running,
and high pitched glee.
You were there in the hushed
tears, silent screams, and echoing
confusion.
The many dimensions of life,
Love, and hate.
You were there, you are here,
you'll always be.
Be mine totally after God
Singular but COMPLETE.

Done with one but onto the NEXT
Buried gold, jewels, diamonds and rubies.
Never too sure, always too inquisitive.
Let silence speak and loud noise fall on deaf ears.
You'll find me there.
Be totally unafraid; free.
Do all I can, while I can...why not?
Forget the years. Time in our definition doesn't exist.
Singular but COMPLETE.

- M.E

DETOUR

"I'm stuck, I'm stuck!!" he
screamed while fighting the many
hands that held him
Held him from falling apart in the
loose seams
From thrusting out of his fragile,
paper-like skin
Then he breathed
Or was it more like a sob? Was it
helpless, were we giving up?
"I'm stuck..." he said while they
held him, spoke to his
consciousness as he came through

To his guileless spirit shining through his eyes
But we held on and I prayed because his fight is bigger than anything that our hands could hold
And in that moment...that was enough.
You aren't stuck...he came to…
And in that moment we all were fighting with you and holding you.

- M.E

HUSBAND

I wonder what your conversations
with God are like
If they're loud and rumbling or
soft and long
I wonder if He shares jokes and
smiles with you
And if you get angry and
unresponsive
If you wait for His last word
If you're like me...impatient and
think you know better than you
run while crying because you
don't

Do you mind how you speak to Him?
Do you care what He thinks?
Do you recognize He exists?
Do you speak with Him at all...?

- M.E

NIGHTMARE

Last night I had the dream feeling again
You know
The one where you're buried and no one hears you
By "you" I mean me
I had the dream that slowly crept into a feeling…
It was real, but I'm still here
Last night carried into this morning and I'm so tired of fighting
What is real? What is figment? Are they the same?
I am buried. No one hears me and I was comfortable there until I couldn't breathe.

- M.E

LIFETIME

My sense of time is warped
Left in the past at the bottom of a
barrel of "me toos"
My sense of time is jagged
With what I could afford to
remember and what the body
won't believe
My sense of time is almost cursed
I'm forcing one in front of two to
make sense
Distinguish familial from enemy,
little girls and boys, new and old,
mind and body

Senses and time that could never get through…what is time when the one who notices it
Can't compute, can't or won't remember. Does it exist?

- M.E

FAMILY

I learned about beauty through
my family and I learned to hide
They would talk about proportion
Both men and women
They'd talk of shade and light,
what was acceptable and what
they disliked
Sometimes I'd laugh because
their talk wouldn't include me but
most of the time
I'd hide

- M.E

RECIPROCITY

I send you beats

Beats from my breath

Beats clamoring from a heart

And you beat it back

Never missing a beat, what does

this sound like?

How does it feel?

We're a rhythm

- M.E

HAITIAN

"Do you know what strength it
takes to survive on rainwater
buried under concrete?"

- M.E

CONTRARY

Funny…gut wrenching with tears falling down my face. So hysterical, I was laughing maniacally with my family. Except "Kat" was actually crying. I noticed and that made me laugh more. We three queens told what we remembered or what we wanted to remember. We block it out like pros. Laughing to forget, laughing to drown out the thoughts that frazzle our minds. "We need counseling!"

yelped L. Cue another roar of laughter. Kat stared at us intently as she put her head in her lap to cry out of shock, despair, and for us. While we were laughing, still trying to drown thoughts, the only power we had when we finally told. And then I realized I was crying—the very thing I was trying not to do.

- M.E

LIFE

It's consistency
It's falling while failing
It's doing it, whatever it is, again
and again, even after you've won
It's not expecting less
Living is hard
Death is easy, sometimes quick
Being is hard
Continue
Social media has made popular to
extravagant birthday celebrations.
I never really enjoyed mine.

Deaths came around them, my mom was stuck in Haiti (2 years during the girl to woman phase of my life), I was forced to face issues of maturating into a young woman without her. I felt if I wasn't progressing every year of my life, what's my purpose? Time is on a continuum, am I better, am I useful, can I pay my bills, do I matter? It is took therapy, God, and family to finally accept the things I couldn't change. However, this year I hope to smile with 32 candles, not for any particular reason, but for the simple fact that I am still here

- M.E

BIRTHDAY

Staying present is the present that
I give myself
Every year when this day rolls
around.
Gifts from loved ones pour in
wrapped in love and bows.
They present their gifts as
questions to help me learn and
grow.
Hi Mel, are you happy?
Is there something on your heart?
Is there something you're
expecting?

Have you nixed the blocks within your mind? I'd surely love to know.

Are your laughs pure and happy? Or does your humor mask something?

Mel, are you truly happy? What's the source of it?

Are you giving what you're called to give? Or are you holding back?

To whom and when and where and why?

Can you gaze in the mirror without a sharp pain? Do you like what you see?

Seriously, are you happy?
On my birthday, I unload. I treat myself to the sweet surrender of taking off the mask
That has built and calloused over my being since the last time I stripped myself
And let myself be myself. And know myself.

- M.E

TED TALK

This is where I tell you that I was
raped or molested at the age of
eight
This is when you look at me and
secretly beg my permission to
breathe
You breathe out confusion,
sadness, and anger for a while
And I relive the release of
someone else knowing
While simultaneously hoping
they believe me
And trying to believe myself

This is where I try to push away
any semblance of recollection
Any thought of memories
It's just too DAMN hard
I want to push the work into other
minute things I want to do
I want ease
But this is where my body refuses
me
It's rebelling when I choose to
forget
This is where I tell you I need
help
That I never got a chance to know
my own voice
That I don't trust it outside of its
box

That too much time has lapsed
and I'm still screaming "rebuild,
REBUILD, rebuild!"
Sometimes I need to find my
voice again
And hold onto it
And remind myself that it is still
cherish able and worthy
I am still worthy
I will proclaim my worthiness
every day
Until I see it in the mirror
Until it's how I move
Until I am nothing but
TRUTH!

Twenty three years of running
around in circles
time pausing, rewinding, but not
fast forwarding
fast forwarding at last then lost.
When your innocence is grabbed,
snatched and stolen at the age of
eight
it is difficult to come to terms
with your new truth
that touch is confused with love,
hate, possession, strength and
weakness, too
when I am quiet, I keep running,
run so fast I don't remember

which thought led to another but that's how I keep going because here is where I'm trying to give myself permission to breathe despite the truth.

- M.E

SAY

I said I love you as a joke
Like "ha ha loving is so funny"
Ironic it is
It was laced with sarcasm
Far from truth
It is heavy, sometimes
burdensome, it sacrifices
If you don't have anything left
then
Give yourself

I said I love you as a joke
But secretly I was hurting
I wasn't sure
I should've been sure
But I wasn't I know I should've been since
You were my first home
Mom? No questions now, no doubt
I've had a taste with my nephews
I said I love you as a joke expecting it back
Now I say it to mean it; I say it because it must be true.

- M.E

IF

I ask myself all the time if I am as
great as my parents
They left all they understood
Started from the beginning;
started anew
There are times where I'm
starting with them
And times where they've left me
behind
Is it language, education, or
access?
Is it poverty, ingenuity, or
strength?

Maybe a mixture of what was, what is, and the hope of what will be
If I am like my parents then that is mediocrity maybe worse
But if I am greater, surely there'd be more fanfare
More blessings, less strife but my parents took that less
Made it more
I look to and through loopholes and all the logical reasons of how I answer "why not"

But if I'm like my parents, what
beauty would that be?
To take the possibility of hope
and opportunities
To forge it gold
To remove the blood, the gender,
the cultural shame
Swallow their tongues as they're
drinking filthy water
If I am like my parents

- M.E

MR. TIN-MAN

My own body hid from you
before it seeped into my
subconscious, Mr. Tin-Man
It recoiled, protested, and it was
bothered while it festered
But I operated the blinds,
engineered the satellites, Mr. Tin-
Man
My inside voices protested, held
my mind ransom and soon my
sanity followed,

Mr. Tin-Man
Sprinkled truths into so edible lies
and we both stomached them
Metal, cold, steel, alone and it
was odd to me that you said
you've never been in love, Mr.
Tin-Man
You were missing so much...I
know I was too
Why else would my mirror see
you, Mr. Tin-Man?

- M.E

ME TOO

Well whose fault was it?
Was it mine, was it my cousins'?
Was it the media, the lack of
education, is it cultural?
I have many questions but you
have finite answers, mom.
I still shut my thoughts, close my
eyes, and cement my mouth,
mom.
You so gently play the devil's
advocate,

You say "maybe she could've stopped him...you know call for help.."
But did you hear her yell? Did you see me cry from my day's end into sleepless nights?
Tell me whose fault was it? I long to know so that my yesterdays and my nows don't spill Haphazardly, provokingly into my tomorrows...should I keep the blame?
No...not me, I meant they...

- M.E

ANOTHER TRUTH

I'll share another verity

The biggest one I've learned here

There is no pinnacle

No ultimate, dignified position of influence

They are ALL worthy

If you treasure the tasks

If you find beauty in the faults

If you seek to understand the conundrums

If you aim for peace though all of your work

Do it to the best of your ability and make it happen

Then and only then will you be able to know that your purpose is Intently tied into how you move through life.

- M.E

AGAIN

I discovered it

Through a mistake actually

The best things usually are found

accidentally

I tried again

For more than the sense

More than what I was to know

A feeling really

I kept doing it, going towards new

even though I failed

I know I didn't invent this

But I'm telling you, that's how I'm

surviving

There's life

Again

- M.E

BOTH

Perhaps the strangest thing is that
we can be both
We hold on to both
The dualities of life
The semblance of freedom and
the happenstance of ownership
The look of a cage the reality of
A MIND
Both.
Then maybe one prevails
One is persistent, one fits
Sometimes it's this back and forth

There's a need to choose
Good and evil
Love and hate
Many or one
Life and death.
Both.

- M.E

FLESH

I just see myself going against who
I've professed to be
What I've instructed others to be
And I'm conflicted
With holding on to just the
corporeal; the flesh
Only to find it being the smallest
part of your whole anatomy
The tiniest part of you
Yes it feels good but that's not who
you are
I don't want to lose sight of you
When I'm lost in the feel of you
And we're still looking for our
space.

- M.E

ME

I throw it out forget about it and pick it up again **later**
Hide it in plain sight until it's noticed, I scare it again
Erase it from the only speech I really speak
Give it a patois, create standardized rules
Again again and again
Human scale cycle
Fear of fear, failures and next ups
Mask the ugly, say its beauty
Pain and purpose up and drawn
Again and again and again

- M.E

The past couple of years I've lost more people than I thought I should. I was saddened, then became angry about the losses. Death always brings into question the purpose of life. The people I lost had a lasting impact on the ones left behind; further establishing the belief of life after death and a necessary connection to God.

WELL DONE.

We used to take the same bus. I was going to school and you were returning from work.
I saw you but didn't recognize who you until the day I noticed you giving up your seat for an elderly woman, the next day a pregnant woman, and the next day another passenger...always with a smile. No one saw how tired you were. I recognized your weariness so I offered my seat to you

and you politely declined. And then I saw your smile...Pastor Joe?!

"Wi petite mwen" you said in your native tongue. "Yes my child."

From that day on, we'd chat about our journeys on that bus, about church, about school and about life. I always felt valued when speaking to you. I remember us making light of how emotional you were when we realized we shared a particular trait. I smile because now

I know it is a strength. It is welcomed because it lets me think of you. I never got to say a proper goodbye to you before you returned to the other side of your dear island. I find peace in knowing that where you are now is more beautiful and perfect than anything we can imagine. Rest in His Perfection Welcome Pastor Joe...well done.

- M.E

BROTHER

I looked up and away from the
thoughts that bombard my mind
I saw him across the street
Black hoodie, black sweats, and a
pair of bright red sneakers
coming straight towards me
Tall, lanky, and an air-tight
arrogance about him
I'm glad it was in my hood where
85% of the other young men
dress
Just like him; it wasn't threatening
They all have that "air-tight-
arrogance"

that seems
Bulletproof
Nothing could be farther from the
truth
Truth is...
He's still in his early twenties,
still growth ensues
That air-tight arrogance is the
protection of the plexiglass heart
he has; it must be protected
He still comes home when the
street lights come on to find a bite
to eat and be safely protected in
my father's house
Truth is he's my younger brother;
the last of our clan

But when I saw him across the street he became a black man with all the "responsibility" that it entails
I wanted to cover him, shield him somehow
He got in the car and told me to stop looking "so sad"
But we were in our hood...85% of the other kids dressed just like him
#AltonSterling...

- M.E

www.ingramcontent.com/pod-product-compliance
Lightning Source LLC
Chambersburg PA
CBHW021959290426
44108CB00012B/1140